THE DANGERS OF DRUGS, ALCOHOL, AND SMOKING

THE DANGERS OF ALCOHOL

KRISTIN THIEL

PowerKiDS press
New York

Published in 2020 by The Rosen Publishing Group, Inc.
29 East 21st Street, New York, NY 10010

First Edition

Editor: Jenna Tolli
Book Design: Reann Nye

Photo Credits: Cover Andrew Mayovskyy/Shutterstock.com; series art patpitchaya/Shutterstock.com; pp. 5, 18 Africa Studio/Shutterstock.com; p. 6 Peleg Elkalay/Shutterstock.com; p. 7 Martin Prague/Shutterstock.com; p. 9 Universal History Archive/Universal Images Group/Getty Images; p. 10 George Dolgikh/Shutterstock.com; p. 11 Liam McBurney - PA Images/PA Images/Getty Images; p. 13 Pressmaster/Shutterstock.com; p. 15 Dusan Petkovic/Shutterstock.com; p. 17 Monkey Business Images/Shutterstock.com; p. 19 picture alliance/Getty Imges; p. 21 fstop123/E+/Getty Images; p. 22 Tetra Images/Getty Images.

Library of Congress Cataloging-in-Publication Data

Names: Thiel, Kristin, 1977- author.
Title: The dangers of alcohol / Kristin Thiel.
Description: New York : PowerKids Press, [2020] | Series: The dangers of drugs, alcohol, and smoking | Includes index.
Identifiers: LCCN 2019018547| ISBN 9781725309708 (pbk.) | ISBN 9781725309722 (library bound) | ISBN 9781725309715 (6 pack)
Subjects: LCSH: Alcoholism–Juvenile literature. | Drinking of alcoholic beverages–Juvenile literature.
Classification: LCC HV5066 .T48 2020 | DDC 613.8/1–dc23
LC record available at https://lccn.loc.gov/2019018547

Manufactured in the United States of America

Some of the images in this book illustrate individuals who are models. The depictions do not imply actual situations or events.

CPSIA Compliance Information: Batch #CWPK20. For Further Information contact Rosen Publishing, New York, New York at 1-800-237-9932.

RT
CES

affects a person's
cohol can make it
hard to control your
too much may not do
nd may start to act
nks too much alcohol,
narm to their body, or

t countries. In the
legal age for drinking
important

DANGER ZONE

Different drinks have different amounts of alcohol. One serving of beer is about 5 percent alcohol. One serving of wine is about 12 percent alcohol. Cocktails may be 40 percent or more alcohol.

Alcohol comes in many different forms. Beer, whiskey, wine, and vodka are different kinds of alcoholic drinks.

A SUGARY SUBSTANCE

Alcohol is made when sugars from food are fermented. Fermentation is the chemical breakdown of one **substance** by another. It helps us make many different foods and drinks, but only some of these contain alcohol. **Yeast** works with sugar to make foods like bread and yogurt. Yeast also works with sugar to make drinks, including ones with alcohol.

Adding yeast to sugar starts the fermentation process.

Some types of alcohol are made from foods that taste sweet. For example, wine is made from grapes. Sugar can be found in many foods that don't taste sweet, too. There is sugar in grains, such as rice and barley. When yeast is added to barley sugar, it makes beer.

A LONG HISTORY

People have been making alcohol for thousands of years. There is **evidence** that people discovered how to make alcohol on almost every continent in the world. Researchers have found that people in China made wine out of rice, honey, and fruit over 9,000 years ago. In ancient Greece, a wine made with honey called mead was very popular. Greek writings even have many warnings about drinking too much.

For thousands of years, people also used alcohol as money. The people who built the pyramids in Egypt were paid in beer!

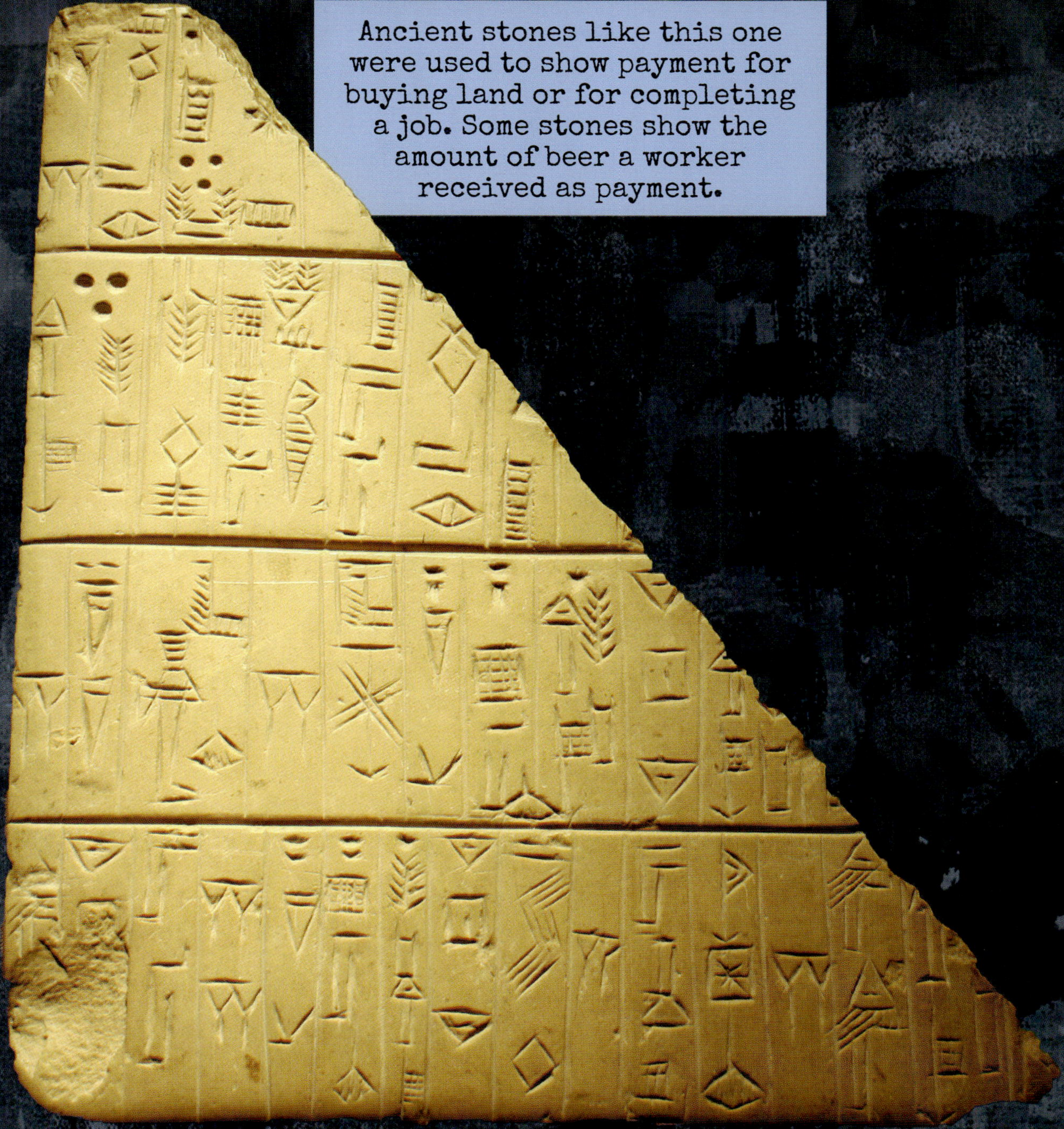

Ancient stones like this one were used to show payment for buying land or for completing a job. Some stones show the amount of beer a worker received as payment.

MOVING THROUGH THE BODY

When people drink alcohol, it moves from the mouth to the stomach to the small intestine. Most of it enters the bloodstream through the walls of the small intestine. Then, the heart pumps blood carrying alcohol throughout the body. When alcohol reaches the brain, it affects the brain's control over thoughts and actions. The liver processes the alcohol and changes it into things the body can absorb, or take in.

DANGER ZONE

Some people think drinking coffee or taking a cold shower helps someone feel less drunk. These are myths. People who drink must wait for their bodies to process the alcohol.

A breath alcohol test measures how much alcohol is in a person's body. Police use this to test if a person drank alcohol before driving.

Everyone is different, but it generally takes about one hour to process one drink. Some tests can find traces of alcohol in the body up to 90 days after the person drank it.

MENTAL AND PHYSICAL PROBLEMS

Alcohol affects the mind and body. It is a **depressant** that can keep people from thinking **logically** and it affects their judgment. People who have been drinking may say or do things they would not normally say or do. They might forget things and have trouble paying attention. They might move more slowly and slur their speech. Drinking a lot of alcohol can cause alcohol poisoning, which can kill people.

Drinking hurts people of all ages, but it is especially unsafe for kids and teenagers. It can cause immediate negative effects, like drops in heart rate. It can also damage organs that are still **developing**, like the brain and liver.

Drinking can quickly cause low blood sugar and low blood pressure in young people. They may pass out, go into a **coma**, or even die.

DRINKING TOO MUCH

Alcohol is not healthy for anyone. However, most adults can safely drink a little alcohol sometimes. **Moderate** drinking is when adults consume one or two alcoholic drinks in one day. If someone drinks too much, they may get a hangover, which means they feel sick hours after they have stopped drinking.

Binge drinking and heavy drinking are two types of **excessive** drinking. Binge drinking is when a woman has at least four drinks in one sitting, or when a man has at least five drinks in one sitting. Heavy drinking is when, in one week, a woman has at least eight drinks and a man has at least fifteen drinks.

DANGER ZONE

Alcoholism is a term used to describe people who are **addicted** to alcohol. Some people cannot control how much they want to drink and can't stop drinking without help.

Alcohol affects men and women differently. The chemistry in a man's body breaks alcohol down faster. Kids' bodies cannot break down alcohol well at all.

PEER PRESSURE

Peer pressure is when friends or people you know **encourage** you to do something. You might be offered alcohol before you are legally old enough to try it. If this happens to you, remember to be independent and make your own choices! Just saying "No, thanks" is enough, but saying no can be difficult sometimes.

Many teens are pressured to try alcohol and other bad things. It can be a big problem for teens in schools and communities all over the country. If someone pressures you to do something you don't want to, they aren't very good friends.

You don't have to say you're sorry for saying no and making your own decisions. Your friends should support you.

RELIGION AND ALCOHOL

Many religions do not allow their members to drink alcohol. But for some religions, consuming alcohol during certain times is part of their traditions. Traditions are services or things that groups of people have been doing for a long time.

The Paulaner monks in Germany brewed beer for centuries. Their beer had alcohol in it along with nutrients that people need to be healthy. They drank it when they fasted and did not eat solid foods.

Christians drink wine during communion, which is a ceremony held during church services. During church ceremonies, people under the legal drinking age may be allowed to drink a sip of wine if their parents approve. Wine is also an important part of the Passover seder, which is a dinner in Jewish households during the first night of Passover.

they will drink less or
ey might start to look
heir eyes are red or
ged.
ose signs in a friend
an adult you trust.
what to do next.

DANGER ZONE

People who start drinking when they are kids are more likely to have problems with alcohol when they are adults.

There are different ways to get help for alcohol problems. Doctors, therapists, and support groups can help someone who wants to stop drinking. A therapist is a person who helps people with mental and emotional problems.

UP TO THE CHALLENGE?

You might not be thinking about using alcohol yet, but you might see others using it. The adults in your family may drink alcohol, or you may know kids who have tried it. You may see it being used on television, too. It is important to know that even a small amount of alcohol can change a person's brain and body.

You can decide not to try alcohol until you're old enough. Then, you can decide to be smart about how much you drink and when you drink. If you are worried about someone's drinking or think they may have a problem, talk to an adult you trust.

GLOSSARY

addicted: Being unable to stop using a drug.

coma: A state in which someone who is sick or injured is unconscious for a long time.

depressant: A drug that makes the body's systems less active.

develop: The act of building, changing, or creating over time.

encourage: To try to make someone more likely to do something.

evidence: Something that shows that something else is true.

excessive: Having too much.

logically: Understanding or thinking about something in a correct or reasonable way.

moderate: Not too much or too little.

permanent: Lasting a long time or forever.

substance: A material of a certain kind.

yeast: A single-celled fungus used to make dough rise and to make alcoholic beverages.

INDEX

WEBSITES

Due to the changing nature of Internet links, PowerKids Press has developed an online list of websites related to the subject of this book. This site is updated regularly. Please use this link to access the list: www.powerkidslinks.com/das/alcohol